William M. Gaines's
THREE RING
MAD

ALBERT B. FELDSTEIN, Editor

A SIGNET BOOK from
NEW AMERICAN LIBRARY
TIMES MIRROR
New York and Scarborough, Ontario
The New English Library Limited, London

★★★★★★★★★★★★★★★★★★★★★★

 Ladies and Gentlemen . . .
And Children of All Ages . . .
Presenting . . .
OUR CLOWNING ACHIEVEMENT . . .

THE
3-RING
MAD

SEE The Strange Freaks of Madison Avenue performing in "MY FAIR AD-MAN"

SEE The Death-Defying Contrived Situations employed in "AN ALFRED HATCHPLOT MOVIE"

SEE MANY OTHER WORLD-FAMOUS ACTS OF IDIOCY ALL SPOTLIGHTED UNDER ONE RIDICULOUS COVER.

YOU'LL roar at the underhanded juggling used in "PICTURES THE EDITORS LEFT OUT"!

YOU'LL applaud the fee-splitting shenanigans exposed in "DOCTOR'S PROGRESS"!

And mainly . . . you'll discover that Barnum was right when he said "There's a sucker born every minute!" . . . Because at this minute, you're it! You just paid good money for

THE 3-RING MAD

★★★★★★★★★★★★★★★★★★★★★★

CONTENTS

DOC HOLIDAY sometimes uses a small Derringer which he hides in his boot!

MARSHAL MATT DILLON prefers the standard-size single-action Colt .45!

WYATT EARP fancies his unique 12" giant, the famous "Buntline Special!"

BUT IF IT'S THE RIDICULOUS
YOU'RE LOOKING FOR
WHEN IT COMES TO TV WESTERN WEAPONS,
THE CHARACTER
THAT'S GOT THEM ALL BEAT
IS
THE IDIOT WHO USES . . .

THE
RIFLE,

MAN!

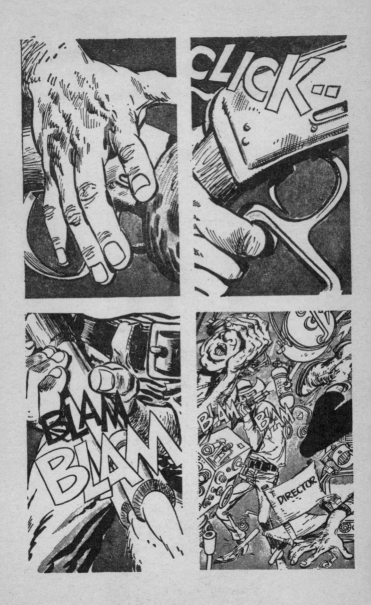

9

10

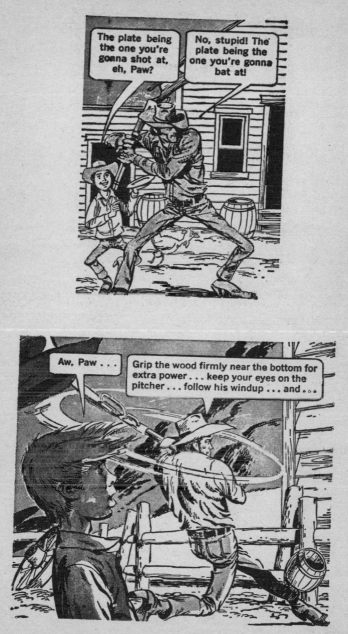

13

15

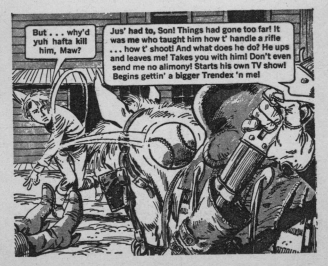

END

Any stranger in this country who reads the wedding and engagement pages in our daily newspapers must be under the impression that: (1) ALL brides and grooms have fancy names, (2) ALL grooms are either members of royalty, doctors, or officers in the armed forces, (3) ALL brides and grooms have attended exclusive, swanky schools, and (4) ALL brides wear fabulous gowns and always carry flowers like orchids and stephanotis (which sounds like a disease to us, and is probably why so many of those brides marry doctors.) Anyway, gang, here we show you a typical…

SOCIETY PAGE

STEPHANIE DUPREY NAPOLEON VII WED IN GRAND CANYON

Miss Stephanie Duprey, daughter of Mr. and Mrs. Eustace Greystoke Duprey XXIV, of Newport, Westport, Bridgeport and Pitkyme Avenue, was married this afternoon to Napoleon VII. He is the son of Napoleon VI and Josephine VI, the grandson of Napoleon V and Josephine V, and a direct descendant of Napoleon I, all of whom reside in the Shady Rest Home for Weary Minds, Hastings - on - Hudson, N.Y.

The ceremony took place in the Grand Canyon to accommodate the unusually large turnout of

Elizabeth Ann Sessingfors wed to Major General Francis Nottingham

20

guests that included the Turkish Army, the Canadian Northwest Mounted Police, the entire Population of Norway, and Elsa Maxwell.

Mr. Dupreys escorted this daughter, who carried orchids and stephanotis, and wore a long-sleeved gown of ivory silk satin studded with real uranium ore. Mrs. Duprey walked directly behind the bride and wore a Geiger counter.

Augustine Snootpelt June Bride of Dr. Maurice Asterbilt

Miss Augustine Snootpelt, daughter of Duke and Duchess Richard Snootpelt, of Coney Island, was married today to Dr. Maurice Asterbilt, son of two parents who hold such exclusive positions in Society that their names are unlisted.

The bride wore a gown of off-white silk organza with a fitted bodice of re-embroidered Alençon lace. Her fingertip veil of tulle was attached to a wreath of orange blossoms over a field of beige oil well deeds. The bride carried a bouquet of orchids and stephanotis.

After a three-year honeymoon

at the Hanging Gardens of Babylon, the couple will take a five-year honeymoon in Newport, R. I., where he specializes in medical practice in diseases of the thumb-nail.

Mrs. Maurice Asterbilt, the former Augustine Snootpelt.

Mr. and Mrs. Napoleon VI at Grand Canyon Ceremony.

The bride graduated from 27 exclusive schools, flunking out only at Bryn Mawr, where she neglected to wear a middy blouse for Friday assembly.

The bridegroom is President of Standard Oil Wells, Consolidated Diamonds, Imperial Plutonium, and the Arnold Stang Fan Club.

In a palace near the statue of Zeus at Mt. Olympia, Miss Elizabeth Ann Sessingfors, daughter of Mr. and Mrs. Oscar Sessingfors, members of the New York Stock Exchange, and owners of the Caspian Sea and the Rocky Mountains, became the bride of Maj. General Francis Nottingham, owner of the 17th Infantry Division.

Mrs. Sessingfors escorted his daughter, who wore a gown of white satin made with a fitted bocice with a scooped neckline and a bouffant skirt terminating in a chapel train. The wedding was delayed for three weeks, due to the late arrival of the stephanotis which came by camel train from Alexandria.

After a brief honeymoon at the Mausoleum at Halikarnassus, the groom, an an alumnus of Harvard, Princeton, Eton, Cambridge, Oxford, and Boody Jr. High School, is planning to sell his infantry division and retire.

The groom is a distant descendant of Adam.

Gen. and Mrs. F. Nottingham after Military Wedding.

Princess Daphne of Bavaria the former Daphne Aldershot

Announce Daphne Aldershot-Prince of Bavaria Nuptials

Mr. and Mrs. Lancelot Aldershot III, of 685 Park Avenue, announce the coming nuptials of their daughter, Daphne, to H. R. H. Prince Izaakian Metternich Dupois y el de Vosmik, son of King and Mrs. Mermio Metternich Dupois y el de Vosmik, of Gemütlich, Bavaria.

The bride-to-be attended Vassar, Wellesley, Finch, the Sorbonne, Juilliard, Seesee-Eawye, and took sewing lessons in the Taj Mahal. The future groom, a direct descendant of Alexander the Great, is a senior at Oxford, where he is majoring in Cashing Large Checks.

The nuptials will take place next May in the south-by-southwest wing of the family inclement weather castle, near Pfefflefinger-am-Rhine, Bavaria.

SOCIETY PAGES LIKE THAT GOT US TO THINKING. WHAT WOULD

HAPPEN IF INSTEAD OF DEVOTING ALL THEIR SPACE TO THE

SNOBS WHO CONSTITUTE 2% OF OUR POPULATION,

THEY DEVOTED THEIR SPACE TO THE SLOBS

WHO CONSTITUTE 98% OF OUR POPULATION!

TO SHOW YOU WHAT WE MEAN, HERE IS . . . .

MAD'S

SOCIETY PAGE

Zelda Zyttzger wed in Bayonne, New Jersey, to Weight Guesser

Miss Zelda Zyttzger, daughter of Mr. and Mrs. Mike Zyttzger, of Bayonne, N.J., was married this afternoon to Sparky Gahagan. He is the son of Mr. and Mrs. Oofie Gahagan, socially prominent Brooklyn old newspaper collectors.

There was a reception at the home of the bride's parents before the wedding, where Miss Zyttzger was introduced to Society. He was Ira Society, a cousin of the groom, and he acted as best man.

The bride is a graduate of the Bertha Kopfelman Elementary School, in Jersey City, where she was an inkwell monitor and schoolyard blackboard eraser clapper. She is currently attending the Max Kolodny candy store

in Bayonne, where she studies song sheets.

The bridegroom is an alumnus of the Willie Follack Meat Cutting Institute, President of the Ralston Straight-Shooters, and

Mr. and Mrs. Sparky Gahagan, she is the former Zelda Zyttzger.

is currently a weight-guesser in fashionable Coney Island.

Following a brief honeymoon in Canarsie, the couple will take a bus to Flushing, where they will establish residence.

Fanny Gretch, Jersey Debutante is bride of Manhattan Pugilist

Miss Fanny Gretch, daughter of Mr. and Mrs. Bronco Gretch, of Bronco's Sunoco Station and Clean Rest Rooms, Hoboken, N.J., was married this afternoon to "Boom-Boom" Blattner, son of Mr. and Mrs. Rocky Blattner, of the noted Manhattan sidewalk pretzel salesman clan.

Mr. Gretch gave his daughter in marriage. She was attired in a gown of white taffeta, made with a bateau neckline, and wore what looked suspiciously like white-tinted G.I. combat boots.

Miss Gretch is a graduate of Maxine Litner's Private Kindergarten and attended televised Arithmetic classes in her living room last March, interrupting her course during the finals to switch channels to "Queen for a Day."

23

Announce Birdie Hogan-Lefty Schleck Nuptials in Bronx

Mr. and Mrs. Gus "Roughouse" Hogan, of Hogan's Fish and Fruit Market, 130 Fulton Street, announce the coming nuptials of their daughter, Birdie, to Lefty Schleck, son of Mr. and Mrs. Ziggy Schleck, of Ziggy's Bar and Grill, 176 Mott Haven Blvd.

The bride-to-be attended P.S. 215, P.S. 177, P.S. 14, P.S. 109, and Dora Schiffler's Mambo Studio.

The future groom, a direct descendant of bookmaker Snooky Schleck, is currently studying for his High School diploma at home. Which is one on him, since he never graduated from Public School!

The nuptials will take place on April 17th, at the Paradise Cha Cha Club of the Grand Concourse, providing the annual Mah Jongg Round Robin and "Go Fish" Card Party of the Classy Bronx Ladies Club is over in time.

Goldie Zelch December Bride of Goon Furd

The former Miss Goldie Zelch.

Miss Goldie Zelch, daughter of Mr. and Mrs. Ninny Zelch, of Ninny's Carting and Haulage Co., 76 Hester Street, was married today to Goon Furd, son of Mr. and Mrs. Fatso Furd, the highly prominent West Side chicken pluckers.

The bride wore an off-white

Sophie P. Plettz weds Private First Class Lefty Hocknock

In a reconverted hardware store near the South Side stockyards, Miss Sophie Phoebe Plettz, daughter of Mr. and Mrs. Yogi Plettz, of the East River junk barge "Sophie Belle," became the bride of Pfc. Lefty Hocknock, a permanent member of the K.P. squad at Ft. Dix, N.J. The bridegroom is the son of Rock Hocknock, stevedore on the fashionable West 48th St. docks.

Mr. Plettz, whose life's savings ran out, while paying for his daughter's wedding, escorted the bride, who wore a gown of ivory satin terminating in a pair of Ked's sneakers. Since her father couldn't afford flowers, the bride carried an armful of multicolored Burpee seed packets.

After a brief honeymoon at Simon and Miriam Boshnick's Vegetarian Utopia House in South Fallisburgh, N. Y., the couple is planning to establish residence at the Ft. Dix guardhouse, where they will await the groom's

The groom is a graduate of Stillman's Gymnasium and is rated 1/78th of the country's 177, nationally ranked middleweight contenders.

After a brief honeymoon in Madison Square Garden, the bridegroom will resume his visits to Dr. Julius Stouffer, of 1401 Broadway, because he gets like a constant ringing in his ears.

Stripper Booboo Adair Wed to Red Getzoff

Miss BooBoo Adair, daughter of and star performer for Mr. and Mrs. Murray "Ironhead" Adair, owners of the Hotcha Burlesque Theatre, was married here today to Red Getzoff. He is the son of Mr. and Mrs. Bernard Getzoff, of the socially prominent Flatbush rag-picking clan.

The bridegroom studied with the New York City Department of Sanitation, where he majored in early morning Can-Clanging. He is currently Director of Undershirt Tearing for the Actor's Studio Wardrobe Department.

Miss Adair is a graduate of Minsky's, the Ziegfield Follies,

Bowery Wedding for Miss Sadie Dooley and Blubber Knerd

Ferdie's Flop House, on Grand Street and the Bowery, was the setting at noon today for the marriage of Miss Sadie Dooley, daughter of Mr. and Mrs. "Two Ton" Dooley, who reside in the doorway of 76 Houston Street, to Blubber Knerd. He is the son of Mr. and Mrs. Nappy Knerd, of Bench 3, 74th Street and Central Park West.

Mr. Dooley escorted his daughter, who was attired in a gown of off-brown Idaho Potato burlap, made with a square neckline, three-quarter length sleeves, and terminating in Thom McAn chukka boots. The bride carried a bouquet of fresh kohlrabi.

Miss Ducky Dooley, sister of the bride, was maid of honor and owing to her well-muscled physique, also served as best man.

The bride and groom, both of whom attended Barney's Billiard Academy, are planning to catch an empty freight car to Miami, where they will honeymoon.

reconverted Lee Overalls ensemble and carried a bouquet of roses, marred only slightly by patches of crab grass. The groom wore a partially lengthened Bar Mitzvah suit, and carried his father, marred only slightly by the contents of the punch bowl.

After a one-week honeymoon in the home of the bride's parents, the couple will move in with the groom's parents, who will probably send them back to the bride's parents.

Following the honeymoon, the groom will resume his important position as first on line to sign for unemployment checks at the N.Y. State Employment Office, 176 Fordham Rd.

court martial trial for being A.W.O.L. to attend his wedding.

The former Sophie Phoebe Plettz.

Yetta Scungilli is Betrothed to Bruno "Baby Face" Slorp

Announcement has been made by Mr. and Mrs. Zippo Scungilli, grape pressers at the Blotto Winery, Modesto, California, of the engagement of their daughter, Yetta, to Bruno "Baby Face" Slorp, son of Mr. & Mrs. Burgundy Slorp, who also

Studios and is currently doing graduate work at Vic Tanny's. She is also a member of Fatties Anonymous.

The prospective bridegroom is a direct descendant of Willie Sutton and attended the famous West 85th Street rumble last April.

The wedding will take place in the late spring, and following the couple's honeymoon in a pala-

the Follies Bergere, and is at present special editorial advisor with Playboy Magazine. Mr. Adair escorted his daughter during the ceremony. The bride wore practically nothing.

END

25

Don Martin, MAD's maddest
artist, who used to be a
short order cook (he would

BREAKFAST

cook a pair of shorts if anybody ordered them), now tells about how he served:

AT LIGGETT'S

END

IT CAME FROM OUTTA THE AD SPACE DEPT.

Have you noticed the rash of "Horror" movies Hollywood is turning out lately? No, we're not talking about "Technicolor-Musical!" Horror movies! We're talking about "B-Picture" Horror movies with monsters in them . . . monsters like "The Fly," "The Blob" and "The Creature From The Black Lagoon!" Well anyway, these Horror movies are pretty popular. Which is leading to a big problem: namely, the producers of these movies are running short of new ideas for monsters! So here is MAD's answer: all Hollywood has to do is take a good look at the work Madison Avenue is doing along the same lines, and their problems are solved. Then, before long, we'll all be seeing movie posters like these . . . advertising . . .

NEW

MOVIE MONSTERS

from

MADISON AVENUE

SEVEN DAYS THAT
SHOOK THE BEACH
SEE THE SPINE-TINGLING TRANSFORMATION!
FROM 97-POUND WEAKLING TO
SAND-KICKING BRUTE

THE DYNAMIC
CHANGELING

PRODUCED BY: DIRECTED BY:
CHARLES ATLAS   VIC TANNY
                          STARRING:
ORSON BEAN (as "The BEFORE")   VICTOR MATURE (as "The AFTER")
WITH LYLE BETTGER (as "The BARBELL") AND A HARD-PRESSED CAST

IT TORE UP THE NATION'S HIGHWAYS

THE CLUTCHING TREAD

IT STARTED IN NEW YORK AND PLOWED ITS INEXORABLE COURSE ACROSS THE COUNTRY TOWARD THE LOS ANGELES FREEWAY, DEFYING THE SPEED TRAPS, IGNORING THE ROAD SIGNS, DESTROYING ALL IN ITS PATH! THE MANIACAL INVENTION OF DOCTOR IGNATZ Q. ARMSTRONG, A DISGRUNTLED PEDESTRIAN!

LEARN THE AWFUL SECRET OF THE STRANGE BLACK DISCS
SEE THE AAA'S FUTILE ATTEMPTS TO HALT ITS PROGRESS
THRILL TO THE EXPLOSIVE CLIMAX ON A DEAD END STREET

MEN GASPED! WOMEN SCREAMED!
CHILDREN WONDERED!

IT WAS THE GREATEST HORROR OF ALL TIME!

THE INCREDIBLE LIVING BRA

STARRING:
Selma Maidenform
Herman Questionmark
Penelope Playtex

And a firm supporting cast

"Never lets down till the final scene!"—The News
"A breathtaking and uplifting experience!"—The Mirror
"Tense . . . taut . . . gripping excitement!"—The Times

IT WAS DRUNK WITH POWER!

THE
TERROR
FROM THE EARTH'S CORE

WHY DID ITS UNQUENCHABLE THIRST DRIVE IT TO THE SURFACE?
WHY DID IT COME TO DRAIN THE EARTH OF ITS LIQUID RESERVES?
WHY DID IT CLAIM THE FIFTH WHEN IT GOT TO WASHINGTON, D.C.?
WHY WOULD YOU EVER CONSIDER PAYING TO SEE THIS AWFUL BOMB?

See the awful day TERROR stalked the earth!

THE INVASION OF THE GREEN GIANT

THIRTY STORIES OF CRAZED CHLOROPHYL!

A MAD MOUNTAIN OF FRENZIED FOLIAGE!

SEVEN THOUSAND TONS OF RAMPANT RHUBARB!

AND NOTHING COULD STOP IT . . .
NOT EVEN WEED KILLER!

"Corny!"—The Herald Tribune

"They should have kept it in the can!"—The Journal American

"Shrivelled on Hollywood & Vine!"—The Chronicle

"A lot of crop!"—Arkansas Gazette

YOU'LL WAKE UP SCREAMING...FROM....

"THE CREATURES IN THE MATTRESS"

WHAT HIDEOUS MISSION WAS THIS ARMY OF TINY MONSTERS SENT TO CARRY OUT?

STARRING:

SPRING BYINGTON   FIDEL CASTRO   JEAN SIMMONS   AND A TIRED CAST

"I tossed and turned in my seat!"—Kravitch, STAR   "We're bedding on this one!"—GAMBLER'S GAZETTE

"Could be a real sleeper!"—EVENING POST   "Good night!"—DAILY POOP

END

LIGHT SWITCH DEPT.

When Ben Franklin began fooling around with his kite, trying to discover electricity, we're sure he had much more worthwhile things in mind for Mankind, than its eventual use in the "spectacular" type of outdoor electric sign. But, thank goodness for Mankind, there's a kind of poetic justice in every abuse of a good thing. And these fancy night time advertising displays are no exception. Because, although they can be garish and annoying, they can also be a million laughs . . . mainly when some of their bulbs and tubing burn out. Here, f'rinstance, are some examples of electrical boo-boos that point up a few of the

HAZARDS OF ILLU- MINATED SIGNS

YOU CAN BE
SURE
IF IT'S
WESTINGHOUSE

YOU CAN
SU E
IF IT'S
WESTINGHOUSE

FLY NOW—
PAY LATER
via **TWA**

FLY
LATE
via **TWA**

WINSTON
TASTES GOOD
LIKE A CIGARETTE
SHOULD

WINSTON
TASTES
LIKE A CIGAR

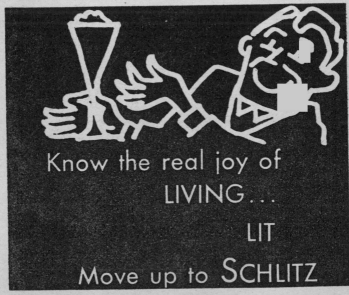

CUNARD LINES

GETTING HER IS
HALF THE FUN!

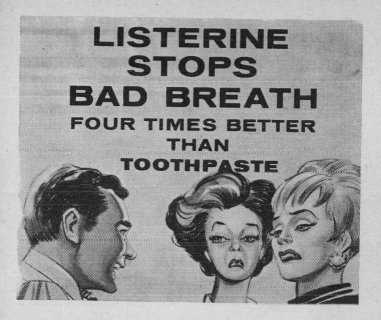

**LISTERINE
STOPS
BAD BREATH**
FOUR TIMES BETTER
THAN
TOOTHPASTE

**LISTERINE
TOPS
BAD BREATH**
U S E

TOOTHPASTE

THE MAN WHO THINKS
FOR HIMSELF KNOWS...
ONLY **VICEROY**

has a thinking man's filter...
a smoking man's taste!

54

MAD
MAGAZINE

EC CH

END

ROUTE OF ALL EVIL DEPARTMENT

Since this is the time of year when the highway accident rate normally goes up... and since we figure you're more likely to continue to buy MAD if you stay alive, we now present...

MAD'S TIPS ON HIGH SAFE

W A Y
TY

If you become drowsy while driving,
pull over to side of road for a nap.

Be sure to inspect your tires every
1000 miles for damage or tread wear.

Do not attempt to pass cars on hills
or curves where vision is obstructed.

Highway signs were placed there for
your protection. Read and obey them!

Monoxide gas is deadly. Always open garage doors before starting engine.

Slow-moving traffic should keep to the extreme right lanes of highways!

Never pass a school bus when it has stopped to load or unload children.

At all 4-way stops, the motorist to the right always has the right-of-way.

For high-speed driving, large, heavy cars are more roadworthy, hence safer.

When road conditions become hazardous from ice, sleet, or snow, always stop immediately and install tire chains.

Always crimp front wheels against the curb when parking on a hill as an added precaution against brake failure.

On narrow, winding roads, sound your horn at each blind curve in order to warn oncoming cars of your approach.

If you must drive at night, make it a practice to stop every 100 miles for a few minutes of diversion to prevent monotony and its resultant drowsiness.

Running out of gas on a turnpike or freeway can be dangerous! Be sure you have an adequate supply of fuel when entering a "limited access" highway!

Driving on poorly marked roads can be dangerous. Always stop and make local inquiry about road conditions before attempting to leave the main highway.

Most accidents occur at night. If you take a long trip, plan to drive during hours when sunlight is adequate.

Drinking and driving do not mix! If
you must drink, play safe. Leave your
car parked where it is, and walk home!

Seat belts can prevent serious injury
in case of an accident. Install them
NOW! It's worth your peace of mind!

END

MAD GOES TO AN

ALFRED HATCHPLOT

MOVIE

Did you ever wonder where Director Alfred Hatchplot gets the ideas for his exciting suspense movies? We got news for you: he takes them from plain ordinary every-day events! In fact, the plainer, the ordinary-er, the everyday-er the event, the more exciting and suspenseful the picture! F'rinstance, take the dullest everyday event you can possibly imagine. Namely, an average clod mailing a letter ·

Pretty dull, eh? Pretty sickening,

wasn't it! Wait!

Here's what happens

to the very same everyday event

when Alfred Hatchplot

gets ahold of it!

71

73

Of course not! Who'd be idiotic enough to name a beautiful girl like this "Sidney"? Her real name is "Melvin"! You see, being a Hatchplot movie, Melvin . . . I mean Sidney, actually Melvin, is a U.S. agent working for the enemy, but really working for us while working for them. See, she starts out as a good guy, but turns into a bad guy, and makes us think she's good by acting bad, which she is . . . Good, not bad!

In other words, I'm a bad good guy, and not a good bad guy, because next to good goodness, bad good ness is better than bad badness! Especially in Alfred Hatchplot movies!

Whew! Would you mind very much if I got off here, and continued my trip by plane?

82

END

ANCIENT HISTORY TELLS US THAT ROME
BECAME THE MOST POWERFUL EMPIRE IN THE
CIVILIZED WORLD. AND THEN THE ROMANS
STOPPED WALKING, AND TOOK TO RIDING
ABOUT IN CONVEYANCES. AS A RESULT OF
SELF-INDULGENCES SUCH AS THIS, THE
ROMANS BECAME SOFT AND FAT. AND SO THEY
WERE EASY PUSH-OVERS FOR THE LEAN
AND HUNGRY BARBARIAN INVADERS
FROM THE NORTH.

TODAY, THE UNITED STATES HAS BECOME THE
MOST POWERFUL NATION IN THE CIVILIZED
WORLD. AND LIKE THE ROMANS, WE ARE
BECOMING SELF-INDULGENT. F'RINSTANCE,
LITTLE BY LITTLE, WE HAVE STOPPED
WALKING, AND TAKEN TO RIDING ABOUT IN
CONVEYANCES. AND SO, AS A RESULT,
MAD FEELS THAT . . .

AMERICA
IS
GETTING
SOFT

In the old days, when we needed something at the grocer's we walked. Today, we drive to the supermarket in our cars.

Our kids don't even walk to school any more. A bus picks them up at the corner, or Mom drives them the two blocks.

Climbing stairs was once good exercise. Today, the only stair-climbing we do is when the elevator's out of order.

And in places where elevators would make no sense, like a two-story building, we've replaced stairs with escalators.

LITTLE BY LITTLE, ELIMINATING THE

There was a time when the average, inactive businessman got his exercise out on the golf course, walking around the 18 holes. Today, he rides around in a "Golfmobile".

The inactive man also used to get exercise pushing a lawn mower. Today, the gadget is mechanized. Now, he sits at a desk all week, and sits at the lawn mower on the weekend.

WHAT—ME WORRY?

BRING BACK MUMBLE-DE-PEG!

CONVEYANCES ARE NEED FOR WALKING

The necessity of walking is being eliminated from other sports, too. F'rinstance, skiing. A skier once got good exercise climbing them ski hills. Now, he uses ski lifts.

Recently, the greatest threat of all, mainly the one that threatens to eliminate walking entirely, made its appearance. THE MOTOR SCOOTER! To see its effect, turn page:

THE MOTOR SCOOTER WILL ELIMINATE ALL LEG-WORK

IN OUR SPORTS

BASEBALL

America's National Pastime will take to wheels as crowds cheer a new version of the home run   the "home drive"

FOOTBALL

Our exciting Fall spectacles will feature a new gridiron
star, the Quarterback affectionately called "snake axles".

BASKETBALL

College and Professional Coaches will search the country
for men who can shoot baskets while driving tall scooters.

IN OUR DAILY LIVES

Social dancing will have the new look as ballrooms become death traps for couples who aren't light on their wheels.

Americans will become so lazy, they won't even walk from the front door to the garage for the car; they'll scooter.

Motor scooters will be carried everywhere, hanging from the back of the family car like a dinghy on a motor yacht.

And as infants grow up in this lazy, self-indulgent world, they'll be taught to scooter instead of learning to walk.

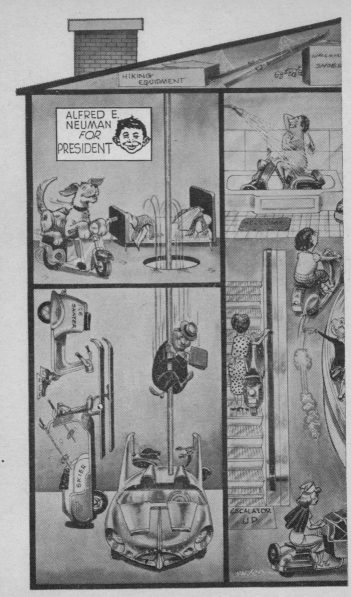

The American home will be re-designed for the family on wheels. The patter of little feet will no longer be heard

around the house. Instead, we'll hear the screeching of brakes and the clatter of engines as walking disappears.

In time, our legs will become vestigial organs, and we'll end up soft and fat, looking like round-bottom toy dolls.

And round-bottom toy dolls, like the Romans, will be easy push-overs for the lean, hungry barbarians from the East.

END

Lately, our maddest artist, Don Martin, has been fascinated with magic. It all started when he got married and learned that the hand is truly "quicker than the eye." Mainly, his wife started grabbing the MAD checks before he even saw them!

THE MAGICIAN

END

There seems to be a rash of new musicals slated for Broadway based on the "Madison Avenue" theme. Since one of the most successful musicals ever to hit Broadway was "My Fair Lady," based on the book by George Bernard Shaw, we figure it won't be long before we'll be seeing a hit "Madison Avenue" musical along the same lines and called . . .

My Fair Ad-Man

BASED ON THE BOOK

"YOU'RE A PIG, MALLION"

BY GEORGE BERNARD SCHWARTZ

ACT 1, SCENE 1: EARLY MORNING ON MADISON AVENUE, OUTSIDE OFFICE BUILDING HOUSING BVD&O, A LARGE ADVERTISING AGENCY. ENTER OFFICER EINSFOOT

* I have often walked
Down this street before;
Taking graft could be like
    any other beat before;
Ah, but nowadays,
Only soft sell pays
When your beat's on the street
    of the ads.

People stop and stare
At the colored signs
Telling them to buy their beer from
    Schlitz and beans from Heinz;
That is how I make
My share of the take;
Writing schmaltz for the street
    of the ads.

*Sung to the tune of: "On The Street Where You Live"

101

ENTER HENRY HIGGENBOTTOM AND CHARLES PICKER-WICK, BVD&O ACCOUNT EXECUTIVES ON THE WAY TO WORK . . . FOLLOWED SHORTLY BY IRVING MALLION, A BEATNIK . . .

... and that's the pitch! I figure I'll play it **cool** for a double bill-payer until my gig comes on!

But, Glib Street, Irving! I dig that creative cats have to be bugged till they make it, but this Madison Avenue bit is, like, too far out!

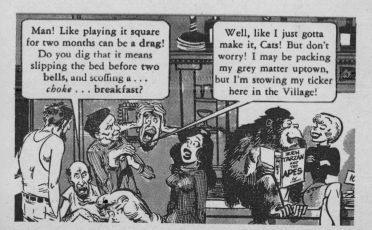

Man! Like playing it square for two months can be a drag! Do you dig that it means slipping the bed before two bells, and scoffing a ... *choke* ... breakfast?

Well, like I just gotta make it, Cats! But don't worry! I may be packing my grey matter uptown, but I'm stowing my ticker here in the Village!

112

ACT 2, SCENE 1: THE NEXT MORNING. HENRY HIGGEN-BOTTOM AND CHARLES PICKERWICK DISCUSS THE PREVIOUS NIGHT'S EVENTS IN HENRY'S PLUSH OFFICES AT BVD&O . . .

114

I was hoping you'd feel that way! Now, I know we're on the right track! But, to look like an ad-man is one thing! To think like one is another! I will now teach you the most important basic principle we have here on Madison Avenue!

Repeat after me . . .

An ad that's bad will end up spoofed in MAD! *

An ad that's bad will end up spoofed in MAD!

Again!

An ad that's bad will end up spoofed in MAD!

I think he's got it! I think he's got it!

An ad that's bad will end up spoofed in MAD!

*Sung to the tune of: "The Rain In Spain"

117

I can't see why you're so unhappy, Henry! You've won your wager. Mallion was introduced as the head of our Los Angeles copy department, and no one suspected a thing!

That's just it, Pickerwick! We did too good a job on the poor lad! Did you see him, shaking hands with everybody, agreeing with things we know are so completely contrary to his nature. We did him a gross injustice! We ruined him! We found him fresh and clean . . . and we . . .

Fresh and clean?

Yes! Not in the physical sense, perhaps, but his mind was fresh and clean, free of the falseness of our world. And we threw him into it . . . chin deep!

Good morning, Henry, Charles! If you have a moment, I'd like to discuss our little experiment!

Don't bother, Mallion! We understand completely! I want you to know that I'm sorry I got you mixed up in this madness . . . and that I'll start making it up to you immediately by calling a publisher friend of mine. Your novel will be printed, and you'll be free to return to your old life as soon as you wish!

121

122

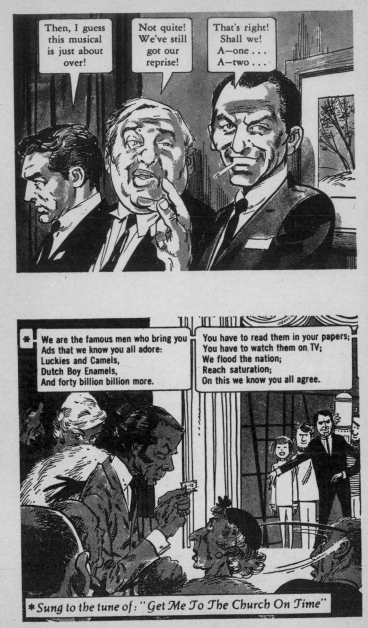

If you don't listen,
    we don't care, friend;
We'll go subliminal
    and get you in the end!

'Cause we are the guys who make commercials;
Here is our stirring battle song:
"We do the lying;
You do the buying!"
And now we bid you all . . .
And now we bid you all . . .
And now we bid you all . . .
So . . . Long.

END

YESTERDAY

WE ARE ALL FAMILIAR WITH THE MARVELOUS ADVANCES THAT MEDICAL SCIENCE HAS ACHIEVED IN THE LABORATORY . . . BUT HOW MANY OF US EVER STOP TO

DOCTORS'

In the old days, distance was a serious problem. Patients often had to cover long miles to reach a doctor, and this resulted in many dangerous . . . and even fatal . . . delays.

TODOY

THINK ABOUT THE MARVELOUS ADVANCES MADE BY
OUR WONDERFUL FRIEND . . . THE FAMILY DOCTOR? IN
THIS ARTICLE, MAD CAREFULLY EXPOSES THE . . .

PROGRESS

Today, the telephone immediately spans long distances and
reaches the doctor's office, where the nurse can tell you
how many days you'll have to wait before you can see him.

In the old days, waiting rooms were small, uncomfortable and offered no diversion, such as magazines, to quiet the nerves of the anxious patients waiting to see the doctor.

Today, the busy physician includes a large, comfortably-furnished, modern waiting room as a part of his offices, which makes the ordeal of getting sick almost a pleasure.

In the old days, the lack of up-to-date medical equipment made it difficult for the doctor to administer properly to the patient who came to him with any serious problem.

Nowadays, excellent equipment is available to the General Practitioner, only he doesn't have it! Instead, he sends his patients to the guys who do . . . THE SPECIALISTS!

In the old days, a day off for a doctor was rare, and if it was taken, was particularly rough on his patients who had no way of reaching him should an emergency case arise.

Today, no matter where the doctor goes, he can remain in constant touch with his office to advise emergency cases which arise that he's operating, and find another doctor!

In the old days, the doctor's bill took a long time to be settled. Mail was slow, and often he forgot to send one, so the patient usually had to remember to pay it himself.

Today, our modern billing methods, fast mail service, and mainly collection agencies, lawyers, and courts make this, the doctor's most important activity, quick and efficient.

END

WHENEVER WORKERS GO OUT ON STRIKE, THEY AN-
NOUNCE THE FACT TO THE GENERAL PUBLIC BY FORM-
ING A PICKET LINE, AND CARRYING AROUND "ON
STRIKE" SIGNS. THE TROUBLE IS, THERE ARE SO MANY
STRIKES THESE DAYS, THE PUBLIC DOESN'T REALLY
NOTICE PICKET LINES LIKE THEY USED TO! MAINLY BE-
CAUSE THESE PICKET LINES WITH THEIR UNIMAGINATIVE
"ON STRIKE" SIGNS ALL LOOK ALIKE! SO **MAD** SUGGESTS
THAT STRIKERS WISE UP, AND CREATE ENTERTAINING
"ON STRIKE" SIGNS THAT PERTAIN TO THEIR PARTICULAR
TRADE OR PROFESSION, AND START FORMING THESE . . .

DISTINCTIVE

PICKET

LINES

FOR RAILROAD WORKERS

133

FOR MOVIE USHERS

The Brotherhood of
Movie Ushers
LOCAL 4597
PROUDLY PRESENTS
"LOOK WHO'S
STRIKING!"
Continuous Performance
Daily

STARRING
Oscar, Ed, Sam,
and Bernie
WITH
Tom,
The Ticket-Tearer

directed by
Union Boss
"Big Jim"
McGraw
produced by
Local 4597's
Strike Fund

AND
INTRODUCING
14
IMPRESSIVE
PROFESSIONAL
PICKETS
Direct from
their last strike

"A masterpiece
of timing! Certain
to ruin the
theatre owner!"
—Throgg
Usher's Weekly

"Should run
rest of year!"
—Sweeney
Labor News

FOR COLLEGE PROFESSORS:

"All wish to be learned, but no one is willing to pay the price." —Juvenal

"Our praises are our wages." —Shakespeare

"Damn with faint praise." —Pope

"Without money, honor is nothing." —Racine

"Money brings honor, friends, conquest and realms." —Milton

"A fair day's wages for a fair day's work." —Carlyle

"Strike while the iron is hot." —Rabelais

"A dollar in a university is worth more than a dollar in jail." —Emerson

eggheads ... deserve a better deal." —Newman.

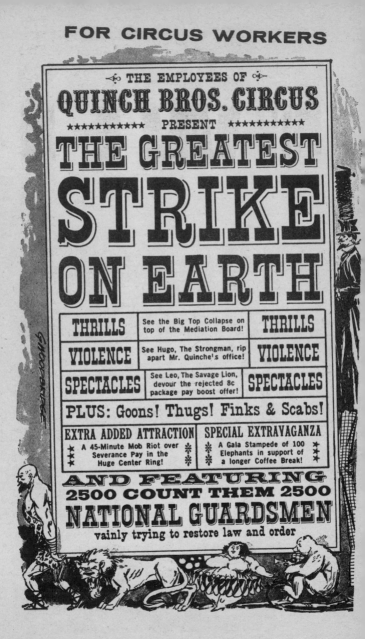

◦ THE EMPLOYEES OF ◦

QUINCH BROS. CIRCUS

*********** PRESENT ***********

THE GREATEST STRIKE ON EARTH

THRILLS	See the Big Top Collapse on top of the Mediation Board!	THRILLS
VIOLENCE	See Hugo, The Strongman, rip apart Mr. Quinche's office!	VIOLENCE
SPECTACLES	See Leo, The Savage Lion, devour the rejected 8c package pay boost offer!	SPECTACLES

PLUS: Goons! Thugs! Finks & Scabs!

EXTRA ADDED ATTRACTION
★ A 45-Minute Mob Riot over Severance Pay in the Huge Center Ring! ★

SPECIAL EXTRAVAGANZA
❁ A Gala Stampede of 100 Elephants in support of a longer Coffee Break! ❁

AND FEATURING 2500 COUNT THEM 2500 NATIONAL GUARDSMEN
vainly trying to restore law and order

END

GETTING A HAIRCUT HAS ALWAYS BEEN A PAIN IN THE
LEFT EAR TO US, ESPECIALLY WHEN THE BARBER NICKED IT
WITH HIS RAZOR. AND SO, WITH THIS ARTICLE, MAD SUG-

In the old days, the local barber shop was
an inexpensive sanctuary for the adult
male, where the bothersome necessity of

GESTS A GIMMICK FOR TURNING AN OTHERWISE UN-
PLEASANT TASK INTO A DELIGHTFUL INTERLUDE, MAINLY
THAT VISIT TO THE LOCAL . . .

getting a haircut was at least offset by
offering an atmosphere free of chattering
women and screaming kids.

Today, however, what with mannish-style hairdos like the Poodle Cut and the Italian Bob, women have invaded the once-forbidden sanctuary known as The Barber Shop. And what's worse, they've brought their children in with them.

The only ones who seem to be enjoying this necessary task today are the kids! In order to distract them, barbers have in-

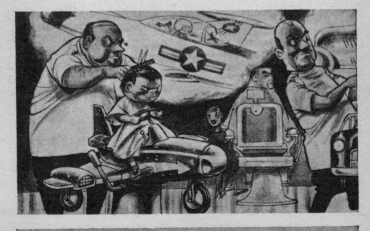

Now turn page to see MAD's suggestion for mak

Yes, the "Police Gazette" is gone from the magazine rack, and the Pin-Up Girl calendar has been taken off the wall. Comic Books and "Vogue" have replaced them. Today, for a man, getting that haircut is a dull, boring waste of time.

troduced special chairs for kids to sit in while they work . . . chairs that resemble horses, and cars, and planes.

ing haircuts enjoyable again for the men . . .

IF IT WORKS WITH KIDS, WHY NOT HAVE

MAD suggests that barbers throw out their traditional barber chairs and replace them with symbols of success, heroism and adventure. Then, getting a haircut would no

SPECIAL BARBER CHAIRS FOR THE MEN?

longer be a dull, boring waste of time — but a twenty-minute flight into adult male fantasy. And best of all, it'll get women and children out of men's barber shops!

END

D'jya ever stop to think about some of the stupid things you say every day? And we're not talking about your opinions or thoughts or ideas, because if you ever stopped to think about them, you wouldn't say 'em. No, we're talking about some of our English idioms, colloquialisms and slang expressions. Mainly, here are . . .

LITERAL TRANSLATIONS

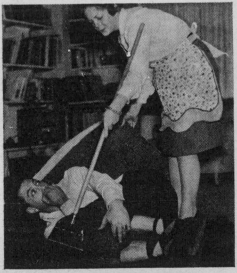

"SHE TREATS HIM LIKE DIRT!"

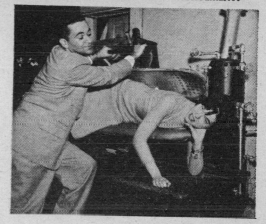

"THEY'VE GOT A PRESSING ENGAGEMENT!"

OF FIGURATIVE
SPEECH

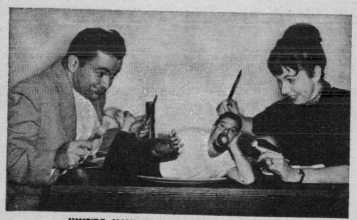

"WE'RE HAVING A FRIEND FOR DINNER!"

"WON'T YOU JOIN ME IN A CUP OF COFFEE?"

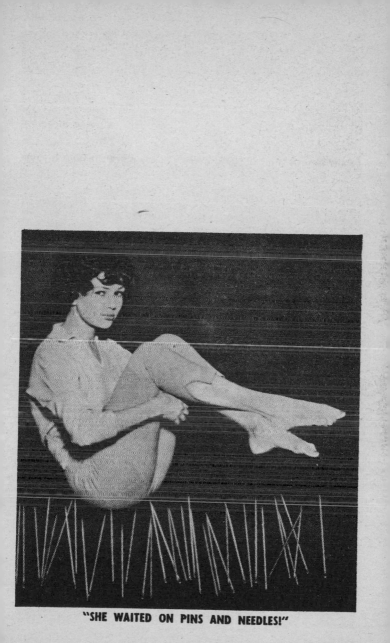

"SHE WAITED ON PINS AND NEEDLES!"

"DON'T BOLT YOUR FOOD!"

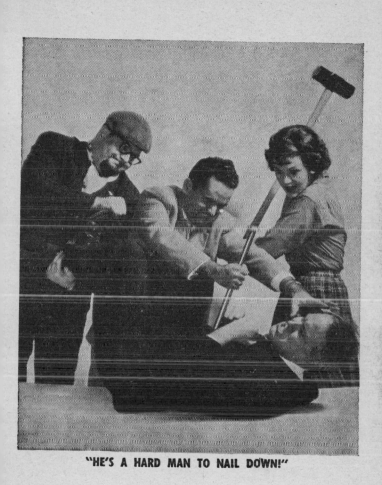

"HE'S A HARD MAN TO NAIL DOWN!"

END

The most important part of running a publication is the job of editing it, which simply means knowing what to **put in**, and what to **leave out**! But most big-time magazine editors are chicken, and often, so as not to offend

PICT

THE
EDITORS
LEFT
OUT

OF THAT
PICTURE-MAGAZINE
ARTICLE

anybody, they leave out the juiciest parts of an article. On this theory, we looked into some recent articles that appeared in well-known picture magazines, and discovered these . . .

URES

F'RINSTANCE, HERE IS A CAREFULLY-EDITED ARTICLE THAT APPEARED IN A PICTURE-MAGAZINE RECENTLY . . .

LICE is there . . . as . . .

Mary Lou Va Voom

WINS

"MISS ENTIRE SOLAR SYSTEM"

TITLE

We follow her through a day hectic with excitement, and we take pictures marvelous pictures that reveal her every thought, her every inner conflict, her every mood, her every emotion, and her every curve.

11:00 A.M. Mary Lou tells LICE reporter that beauty contest can be strong force for moral re-armament!

2:00 P.M. During competition, Mary Lou displays talent up reciting carefully rehearsed speech on "Kindness and Clean Living," hoping judges will respond warmly to it.

4:15 P.M. Mary Lou is proclaimed queen amid wild frenzy as other contestants rush to shower their congratulations.

5:00 P.M. Mary Lou's childhood sweetheart, the boy next door, Melvin Goodslob, proposes marriage right after the contest, and tears well up in Mary Lou's beautiful eyes.

Pictures That Appeared in Article

11:00 A.M. Early-riser Mary Lou tells **LICE** reporter reason she entered competition is to prove to world that beauty contest can be strong force for moral re-armament!

2:00 P.M. During competition, Mary Lou displays talent by reciting carefully rehearsed speech on "Kindness and Clean Living," hoping judges will respond warmly to it.

Pictures Deliberately Edited Out

11:04 A.M. Mary Lou sneaks down to drool at the prizes and dream of how all her friends will just die of envy if she wins them . . . and how she'll just die if she doesn't!

2:12 P.M. Contest judges respond warmly to Mary Lou's recitation, mainly because she punctuates delivery with enchanting movements which she also carefully rehearsed.

Pictures That Appeared in Article

4:15 P.M. Mary Lou is proclaimed queen amid wild frenzy as other contestants rush to shower their congratulations.

5:00 P.M. Mary Lou's childhood sweetheart, the boy next door, Melvin Goodslob, proposes marriage right after the contest, and tears well up in Mary Lou's beautiful eyes.

Pictures Deliberately Edited Out

4:16 P.M. Wild frenzy gets wilder as other contestants' congratulations show they feel far more regally qualified.

5:05 P.M. Tears subside in Mary Lou's beautiful eyes as Melvin gets off her foot. She then informs him that she's accepting Hollywood offer, and leaves with a big producer.

SPORTS ILLUSIONS

honors
THE IDOL
OF THE
NATION'S
YOUTH

"HOME-RUN"
HARNEY

By his exemplary
actions, both on
the field and off,
HOLBROOK
"HOME-RUN"
HARNEY
is inspiring our
youth to greater
athletic
achievements.

158

Picture That Appeared in Article

9:00 A.M. "Home-Run" Harney starts off day working around house, polishes up his Jaguar, claims it's "the greatest car made anywhere."

Picture Deliberately Edited Out

10:00 A.M. "Home-Run" visits an Advertising Agency, poses for Ford testimonial ad which claims it's "the greatest car made anywhere."

Picture That Appeared in Article

1:15 P.M. Appears on pre-game TV program, tells youth of America that he values playing clean, showing good sportsmanship, above all.

Picture Deliberately Edited Out

1:30 P.M. Gets thrown out of game by umpire for using obscene language, gleefully spiking the second baseman, and starting a fist fight.

Picture That Appeared in Article

4:00 P.M. As guest speaker at a meeting of
National Safety Council, advises America's
teen drivers of "safety first" responsibility.

Picture Deliberately Edited Out

4:22 P.M. Rushes from meeting of National
Safety Council, across town, to TV studio to
do benefit for Children's Milk Fund campaign.

Picture That Appeared in Article

4:31 P.M. Harney receives "Elsie" award at Milk Fund show after he advises clean living, and swears he never drinks anything but milk.

Picture Deliberately Edited Out

6:00 P.M. (and into the wee hours), Harney drinks dinner, entertains other sport-lovers at a friendly neighborhood recreation center.

GOOK
MAGAZINE

presents
THE
HONORABLE
VERNON
T
BALOTSTUFER
STORY

HONESTY

INTEGRITY

FAIR PLAY

"There is no
more noble
cause than
to answer
the call to
public
service!"
— *Plato*

Pictures That Appeared in Article

11:00 A.M. Sen. Balotstufer appears before Congress, makes impassioned plea for his slum-clearance bill to help poor in hometown area.

2:15 P.M. As chairman of investigating sub-committee, he chastizes labor leader for such abuses as featherbedding and payroll-padding.

Pictures Deliberately Edited Out

11:20 A.M. He drops in to see how Dad and brothers are doing with new construction company they recently purchased in hometown area.

2:45 P.M. Rushes over to office to disburse own payroll to wife (secretary), uncle (legal adviser), baby (assistant), and dog (typist).

Pictures That Appeared in Article

4:00 P.M. Makes TV appearance for taxpayer group, reaffirms his dedication to fight for economies. less waste in government spending.

6:00 P.M. Tells Gook reporter that Nation's most important freedom, which he would defend to his last drop of blood, is freedom of press.

Pictures Deliberately Edited Out

5:00 P.M. Visits friend, Air-Force General Klod, arranges round-the-world investigation tour for self and family in new B-58 bomber.

12:00 Midnight: Leads a group of supporters as they tar and feather MAD reporter who dug up these photos the magazine editors left out.

END

"The MAD Horror Primer" received such a GREAT response from our readers (i.e. *"A GREAT disappointment!"*—B.F., Phila., Pa.; *"It would be GREAT if you discontinued this type feature!"*—L.D., Dallas, Tex.; *"Articles like that GRATE on my nerves!"*—F.H., Fresno, Calif.) that we've decided to present another primer. This one is for the benefit of any children under seven (in other words, ALL of our readers) who may possibly be interested in working in the advertising field when they grow up.

THE MAD MADISON AVENUE PRIMER

MY FIRST
READER

(EDUCATION-WISE)

Rock-Bottom Slants for Little Group-Noodlers

By Batton, Barton, Durstine
& Cowznofsky

Lesson 1

See the man.
He does advertising work.
He is called an "ad-man".
See his funny tight suit.
See his funny haircut.
Hear his funny stomach churn.
Churn, churn, churn.
The ad-man has a funny ulcer..
Most ad-men have funny ulcers.
But, then, some ad-men are lucky.
They do *not* have funny ulcers.
They have funny high blood pressure.

Lesson 2

See the ad-man run.
Run, ad-man, run.
The ad-man must catch the 8:02.
All ad-men must catch the 8:02.
It is a fast commuter train.
It is never more than two hours late.
And it has a club car.
"All aboard!" says the conductor.
"Chug, chug!" says the train.
"Gulp, gulp!" says the ad-man.
Wouldn't *you* like Bourbon for breakfast, too?

Lesson 3

See the pretty street.
It is called "Madison Avenue".
All the ad-men work here.
They write "Winston tastes good . . ." here.
Write, write, write.
They write "Mr. Clean, Mr. Clean . . ." here.
Write, write, write.
Don't you wish YOU could write like that?
You can.
You're almost *seven* now.

Lesson 4

See the nice advertising agency.
400 nice people work here.
Let us count the 400 nice people.
Count, count, count.
Hmmm! 300 nice people are missing.
The nice advertising agency must have
      lost another nice $4-million account.
Dear, dear, dear.
Where are the 300 nice people now?
At the nice Unemployment Insurance office.
Sign, sign, sign.
Isn't job security nice on Madison Avenue?

Lesson 5

See the kindly old man.
He is the President of the agency.
He has fired 132 people today.
And it isn't even lunch time yet.
Fire, fire, fire.
See the fine young man with him.
He will not be fired, today.
He is a fine ad-man.
He is a fine Vice-President of the agency.
He is a fine son of the President of the agency.

Lesson 6

See the Account Executive.
His accounts are Puffo Cigarettes,
     Bubble Soap, and Flaky Cereal.
The agency loves and trusts him.
Kiss, kiss, kiss.
Trust, trust, trust.
Next week he will resign.
He will form his own agency.
He will have three accounts in his agency.
They will be Puffo Cigarettes,
     Bubble Soap, and Flaky Cereal.
Bounce, bounce, bounce.
That's the way the ball bounces on Madison Avenue.

Lesson 7

See the conference.
Ad-men have 47 conferences a day.
And even more on Sundays.
They discuss EVERYTHING at conferences.
At *this* conference, they are discussing a fire.
It has already destroyed half the agency.
It is now burning up the President's office.
Crackle, crackle, crackle.
What will the ad-men do about the fire?
Soon they will make a BIG decision.
But not at *this* conference.
Perhaps at the *next* conference.

Lesson 8

See the jolly client.
He sponsors a TV dramatic show.
He never finished the 6th Grade.
He can hardly speak English.
He can hardly write his name.
Yet, he re-writes TV scripts.
Re-write, re-write, re-write.
Why do you re-write TV scripts, jolly client?
"Because I do not like sad endings;
Because I only like happy endings."
Someday, a TV writer will shoot the jolly client.
Right in his jolly gut.
What a happy ending THAT will be!

Lesson 9

See the man rate a TV show.
See how he arrives at a scientific rating.
First he makes 10 phone calls.
Then he puts 10 numbers in his hat.
Then he closes his eyes tight.
Then he picks the scientific rating out of his hat.
Oh-oh! This TV show's rating is 6⅜.
Ho-ho! He has made a scientific mistake.
He has picked out his scientific *hat size*.
But it is too late.
It was such a nice TV show, too.
It cost three million dollars, too.
It might have remained on the air, too.
If the man had a bigger head.

Lesson 10

See the amazing average clod.
He is the Eighth Wonder of the World.
He has a 40-year-old body and a 10-year-old mind.
According to Madison Avenue.
So they write TV commercials especially for him.
And they write magazine ads especially for him.
If this keeps up, the amazing average clod will
    become even more amazing.
He will no longer have a 40-year-old body and a
    10-year-old mind.
He will have a 40-year-old body and a
    FIVE-year-old mind.

END

Don Martin, MAD's maddest artist, who hasn't been to a symphony since he got married because now he faces the music at home, recalls for us his last experience at—

THE

CONCERT

END

Just so's you won't get the wrong idea, we want it made clear that we at MAD approve of "Motherhood." After all, some of the world's greatest people—like Shakespeare, Lincoln, Jefferson and Neuman—had Mothers! And we know that these great people thought highly of their Mothers. But, with Mother's Day rolling around again, we got to thinking about the people in history who went wrong! What had these people thought about their Mothers? So, we did a little research on the subject, and came up with a batch of

Mother's
Day Cards

From Some Children Who Didn't Turn Out Very Well

Mother's Day 1778

On this, your very special day,
Have faith in me, dear Mater;
Do not believe them when they say
Your Benny is a traitor!
You'll find some papers with this note
A friend desires to borrow;
You'll know him by his bright red coat;
He'll pick them up tomorrow!

your loving son,
Benedict Arnold

MAY 1926

MOTHER

M is fer da mobsters all around me;
U is fer da underwoild I'm in;
D is fer da drinks I yam bootlegging;
D is fer da doity guy I been;
E is fer da easy life I'm living;
R is fer da rats I gotta pay;
Put 'em all togedder, dey spell
MUDDER...
Youse made me what I yam today!

Your Son,
Al Capone

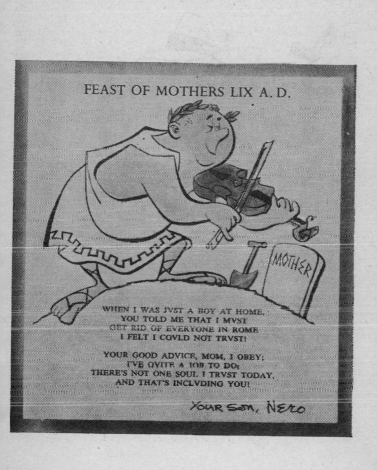

189

MOTHER 1865

My love to you on Mother's Day;
To me, there's no one dearer;
This message must be brief because
The hounds are getting nearer!

Oh—thank you for that birthday gift;
The pistol was a dandy;
Although I've only used it once,
It's really come in handy!

Your Son, John Wilkes Booth

MOTHER'S DAY 1892

When I was just a little child,
You always said I was too wild;
You punished me for all my pranks
And gave my backside forty spanks;
And then, when you were good and done,
Dear Papa gave me forty-one;
I really doubt, sweet Mother dear,
Next Mother's Day, you'll both be here!

Your daughter, Lizzie Borden

Mother's Day 1716

I've flaughtered, tortured, robbed and killed
Until me evil purfe was filled;
I've watched me victims walk the plank,
-And heard 'em gurgle as they fank:
I've flogged a hundred dozen men
And laughed when they fcreamed, "Not again!"
As buccaneer, I bow to none:
Now ain't ye proud that I'm your fon?

love, Eddie "Blackbeard" Teach.

END